A Taste of What's to Come

Lily Lawson

Published by

THE
WRIGHT HOUSE

By the author

Poetry

My Father's Daughter

A Taste of What's to Come

Rainbow's Red Book of Poetry

https://www.lilyswritinglife.com/

Contents

Wine

My first taste of wine, was something quite divine.
I was only 11 at the time. It was white and it was
sweet, a combination hard to beat.   It was something
of a treat. I moved on, as you do, taking a somewhat
broader view. That doesn't mean I have a clue. I
sampled the delights of red, making sure I was
well fed, knowing where empty stomachs led.
Rose called me in good time, to refuse
would be a crime, some of it was
quite sublime. Now my drinking
days
are
few, I
only
buy
the
good
stuff
too,
if you were me, well, wouldn't you?

People

The vivid colours of my life
will never turn to grey.
The multi hues of difference,
forever on display.
The distinctiveness of people,
each single one unique,
it's there within their actions,
and every time they speak.

Easter

Easter being movable
confuses the confusable,
when actually it's easy to work out

Its the Sunday that shall fall,
once the full moon seen by all,
and the first day of spring has come about.

Magic

I am no Harry Potter,
I don't possess a wand,
of taking rabbits out of hats,
I'm really not that fond.

I have no magic potions,
I have no box of tricks,
there are some situations,
that I know I cannot fix.

I do believe in magic,
I know that its real,
beyond the pages of a book,
it's something you just feel.

Book is Open

Write a poem
Write a book
Book of stories
Book a place
Place to set
Place to be
Be yourself
Be original
Original thought
Original ideas
Ideas of who
Ideas of what
What you say
What you are
Are you here
Are you ready
Ready to go
Ready to tell
Tell the truth
Tell us all
All we know
All we feel
Feel the touch
Feel the love
Love the person
Love the work

Work the idea
Work the words
Words convey
Words have power
Power to persuade
Power to tempt
Tempt us all
Tempt us in
In the story
In the door
Door to close
Door to open
Open the book
Open the story
Story ....
Book ....

My Favourite Vase

I have come to rely on you;
your weight, your capacity.
That you will welcome our flowers,
in your height and roundness.
That your heaviness,
that threw me off balance
at our first meeting
is a strength,
belying your fragility?

The intricate patterns of your crystal exterior
reflect the shafts of light
through my window,
casting ever-changing rainbows
in the daylight hours.

In the dark,
you hide your magic,
your secret kept,
until revealed,
by the sun.

The Modern World

Stop all the texts,
remove the mobile phone,
prevent the isolated
spending time alone,
turn off the modem,
cease the internet,
make some memories
you will not forget.

Let Facebook miss you,
let the tweeting stop,
go do your shopping
in an actual shop,
put down the tablet,
put the kindles back,
live dangerously;
read a paperback!

We used to call, to talk,
to just converse,
now it seems
that we find nothing worse.
talking to voicemail
or to answerphone,
we have our conversations
on our own.

Libraries are not wanted now,
close up every door,
dare we venture to wander
or to just explore?
losing real connection,
deprived of human touch,
face to face meetings
have become too much.

Time

Time stands still
sometimes I wish it would,
in the moments of joy,
in the laughter,
in the sharing,
in the hugs.
yet it moves on,
endless, unceasing
so, I try to capture
the memories,
and hold onto them
forever.

When

When the first sight of light breaking
takes the darkness from my sight,
and the dawn of early promise
lights the very blackened night.

When the shadows that you cast
have made themselves just merely known,
and my heart is thumping fast
and all my worries have just flown.

When the waters of the morning
are still silent and so calm,
and the newness of day dawning
seems to shelter me from harm.

When it feels as though my world
forever will not be the same,
and my very self exists
in the utterance of your name.

No tears

No tears, no confetti,
no sparkling champagne,
it's just you and me,
together again.

No limo, no flowers,
nothing to explain,
just us together,
and starting again.

No wedding day jitters,
no rings to exchange,
no music to dance to,
nothing to arrange.

Why can't people get it?
I love you that's all,
I don't want to change it,
we're having a ball.

Goodbye

I don't believe you anymore.
we've been here many times before,
destroying what we had together,
thinking that we were forever.

It's not working anymore,
in the way it did before,
we don't have to stay together,
nothing really lasts forever.

I just can't take anymore.
I know I've said that before,
standing there, saying you love me,
I'm not sure that I love you.

We can't do this anymore,
I have told you that before,
and those words you hurl at me,
I can't believe they came from you.

So, I'm not staying anymore.
I know I should have left before.
you protest that you still need me,
but I've had enough of you.

I don't want you anymore.
I'll live the way I did before.
no matter how you feel about me,
I know I can't be with you.

Truth

It is your truth so you must tell it
It is your choice which words to use
The world is seen through your eyes
Just as it is through mine
Don't confuse the two
they are different
no less true
for all
that

use
your voice
let the world
listen to you
and grasp some small part
of who you really are
if they could see what I see
they would hang on your every word
there would be no other choice to make

Give Me A World

Give me a world
where people all have a home,
where children can laugh
and can play.
Where never is heard
a gun or a bomb,
where diseases are all
kept at bay.

Give me a world
where the people have food,
and there's plenty of water
for all.
Where nobody cares
about colour or race,
where people feel safe
most of all.

Give me a world
when who you choose to be,
is accepted without
any fuss.
Where relationships matter
more than gender or age,
so when we disagree
we discuss.

Give me a world
with access for all,
wherever you're wanting
to go.
Where respect for others
is just understood,
and there is no such thing
as a foe.

Vegas

By the time I get to Vegas I'll be 50,
been standing in the airport line so long.
By the time I get to Vegas I'll be 50,
I'm thinking it might be where I belong.

By the time I get to Vegas I'll be 60,
especially if I decide to take the bus.
By the time I get to Vegas I'll be 60,
suppose you think I'm making too much fuss.

By the time I get to Vegas I'll be 70,
at least I'll have my pension pot to spend.
By the time I get to Vegas I'll be 70,
I'm wondering if my clothes will be on trend.

By the time I get to Vegas I'll be 80,
I have to hope I can still walk the walk.
By the time I get to Vegas I'll be 80,
mind, saying that, I could be all talk.

By the time I get to Vegas I'll be 90,
those bright lights might be too much for me.
By the time I get to Vegas I'll be 90,
the chances are that I'll need company.

By the time I get to Vegas I'll be 100,
either that or I might be dead.
By the time I get to Vegas I'll be 100,
I'll probably have forgotten what I said.

Clear Ahead

Let not our yesterdays,
cloud our vision,
let our today and each tomorrow,
stand alone and count,
may we march onward,
heads held high with confidence,
knowing that everything,
passes us by.

Now you've read my book
don't forget to review
Amazon, Goodreads,
Bookbub too!
Thank you very much
I'm counting on you!

Lily x

Acknowledgements

I would like to thank all the people past and present who have supported me with my poetry by reading, and critiquing and encouraging me.

I am very privileged to have such support.

Thanks to Stuart Honnor for the cover photo.

A few people deserve a special mention –

Christine Hutchinson – for her encouragement and support with all my writing over the years.

Ann Garcia – who continues to inspire me with her poetry, photos, prompts and prose. I value her honesty and support.

Anita Rahlan – for her endless faith in me.

Suzanne Burn - for all the things she has taught me about poetry. I cherish her friendship.

RS - they know why.
(This doesn't count it's not their name)

And finally, my parents for everything they have done for me and given me. Their belief in my poetry means so much.

By The Author

My Father's Daughter

'My Father's Daughter, a collection of poems
ranging from light-hearted to heart-rending
captures Lily Lawson's thoughtful observations
about life and love.'

A Taste of What's to Come

A selection of accessible, relatable, eclectic poetry.
Each piece tells its story in only the way Lily can.'

Rainbow's Red Book of Poetry

Weaving through love and hate,
I rise from the ashes, my words you own –
I am red.

**Something different,
an illustrated children's book.**

Santa's Early Christmas

Last year Santa was hungry and thirsty by the time
he delivered all the presents. But when he came
home there was no food and drink left! This year
Santa decides things are going to be different.

A Poem from My Father's Daughter

Words, Words, Words

Was it to be or not to be?
Were the ides of March a fantasy?
Was it on Twelfth Night it came to be?
Did Macbeth a dagger see?
When Juliet found her Romeo
why did they not take heed and go?
The Tempest raged, brought the terrors,
it was just a Comedy of Errors.
If time means that Love's Labour's Lost
take a Midsummer Dream, hang the cost
Was it King John or was it King Lear?
The one that made the people cheer
Not Desdemona with Othello.
Was she ever with this fellow?
I feel the force of a Winter's Tale,
looking like my time to bail.

About The Author

Lily Lawson is a poet and fiction writer living in the UK. She has poetry, short stories and creative non-fiction published in anthologies and online in addition to her books.

You can find out more about Lily and read more of her work on her blog. Subscribers to Life with Lily are the first to hear all her writing news. You can sign up here.

Printed in Poland
by Amazon Fulfillment
Poland Sp. z o.o., Wrocław

32377985R00027